WILTSHIRE FARMHOUSES & COTTAGES 1500–1850

WILTSHIRE BUILDINGS RECORD

by Pamela M. Slocombe 1988

Monograph No. 1 in a series of selections from the Wiltshire Buildings Record archives.

Publication of this book has been made possible through generous grants from;

The Marc Fitch Fund
The Greene Settlement
The David Knightly Charitable Trust
The Royal Institute of British Architects (Wiltshire Branch)
The McLaren Foundation
Rendell Partnership Developments Ltd
Humberts (Chippenham, Pewsey and Salisbury offices)
The Peter Wakefield Trust
Gaiger Bros Ltd
The Burmah Oil Plc
The Blunt Trust

and through gifts and loans from various members of the Wiltshire Buildings Record.

Plans

All house plans are drawn to the scale 1:250, and direct comparison of sizes is possible. The scale line beneath each plan is divided into metres and the North point is shown. Following the usual convention the front of the house is towards the bottom of the page.

Plans show the buildings at ground floor level. They indicate as far as possible the early forms of the buildings and later extensions and alterations are usually omitted. Staircases are indicated by arrows, former partitions by dotted lines and cellars by crossed lines in the room above.

Key to rooms: H hall, P parlour, K kitchen, S service, D dairy, B brewhouse, SB smoke bay.

Introduction

Discovering the date and history of your house has in recent years become an absorbing pastime for a great many people. There has at the same time developed a need for information about the way old houses are constructed in order that repairs and alterations can be carefully carried out.

This book has been written in order to share with the public some of the findings of the fieldworkers of the Wiltshire Buildings Record since the society, an educational charity, was founded in 1979. During these eight years buildings of all kinds have been examined over a large part of the county but for this first book rural dwelling houses dating from the beginning of the 16th century to the middle of the 19th century have been selected. Buildings in the many small towns of the county have therefore been excluded and so have those in the Southeast quarter of Wiltshire around Salisbury which has been the subject of intensive recording by the Royal Commission on Historical Monuments.

The buildings which are illustrated have come to the Record's attention usually in one of three ways: because of a sale or a planning application to alter or demolish; because of a request by the occupier for the house to be studied; or, in a smaller number of cases, because of a request by the Record to look at the building during the course of a recording day being held in the area.

The random nature of our recording means that we are not in a position to write a comprehensive analysis of Wiltshire's buildings. We felt it would be more appropriate to illustrate with photography some of the building types and features which we have come to realise were in their day quite common in the county but are now less easily found or understood through the passage of time. As far as possible well-preserved examples are shown which may help people to recognise the remnants of similar plans or features. We hope that some of the features which have been omitted through lack of space can be shown in future books in the series.

As much advice as possible has been given about dating, but it must be remembered that every old house will have features from different periods, since major repairs and alterations usually take place at least every hundred years. In order to work out the date of the original building, the dating of several features which can be shown to be part of the basic structure should agree before a conclusion can be drawn. The task is rarely easy, as traditional methods often lingered on for a long time and even the most experienced recorders are continually seeing or learning something new.

Readers should also bear in mind that Wiltshire is one of those counties which has a very high proportion of medieval buildings still surviving. Many must be at present unrecognised to judge from the number that the Record has already discovered. A building often has 16th or 17th century fireplaces and beams which are additions to an older, open hall house. Confirmation of an early date may come only from the roof timbers although it may be suspected because of the type of timber-framing or the wall thickness.

The photographs used in this book have all been taken by

members of the Wiltshire Buildings Record except for one which is an old photograph copied with the permission of the owner. A few of the buildings and some of the features shown have since been altered or demolished. The houses we record are usually occupied and the photographs inevitably show some modern furnishings and fittings which should be disregarded.

The locations of some of the photographs have not been given exactly in order to protect the privacy of the occupiers. Where buildings are specifically named it is because permission has been given or because the building is already well-known. In every case the parish name is stated.

None of the houses shown are open to the public and readers are earnestly requested to consult the Wiltshire Buildings Record if they have an interest in a building rather than attempt to locate it or visit it personally themselves.

The Social Status of Traditional Houses

Rural houses reflect the social structure and geography of the village. A village was not necessarily a single manor. It might contain several hamlets each of which had a 'capital messuage' or manor house. Also the owner of an individual manor might well be living at a large country house some distance away but the capital messuage would still be built to manorial standards and the tenant was accorded the status of chief inhabitant. If the occupier of the house was engaged in the woollen trade as often happened, particularly in the West and Northwest of the county, embellishments to the house could be afforded from his own pocket.

Typical features of capital messuages in the 17th century were decorative staircases, fireplaces and doorways, stone or timber mullioned windows and sometimes plasterwork and panelling. These houses were well built and they have usually survived though often nominally downgraded to Manor Farm, Church Farm or some other name. Their former manorial status can then only be discovered from documentary research.

In the 16th and 17th centuries the demesne lands were usually farmed directly from the manor house. The farmyard with the barn and other buildings would be there. In the 18th century a Manor Farm or Home Farm was often built nearby so that the manor house could have a more elegant setting. The farm would be rather better built than other farms in the village. Sometimes the original manor house became the Manor Farm and a new large house was built for the Lord of the Manor.

The Rectory or Vicarage also had land, the glebe land, and therefore, until the reforms of the 19th century, it usually had an attached farmyard or it, too, had a separate farm which might be called Glebe Farm, Parsonage Farm or Church Farm. This would also be well built but slightly less so than the Manor Farm.

Below this social level were the yeoman farmers and the husbandmen. The yeomen were sometimes freeholders or leaseholders but were often copyholders, in Wiltshire usually holding their farms on three lives. That is, an entry was made in the Court book of the manor that a person held a certain house and lands paying so much a year for the length of the lives of three named people, one of these was often a child so that the holding was assured for a long time. Yeomen sometimes also worked in the woollen or other trades in which case they had much more disposable income to spend on their houses and possessions. Some were the younger sons of good families. Their houses were usually along the village street and their lands were scattered in the common fields. When the final stages of enclosure took place in the 18th and 19th centuries some new farmhouses were built away from the villages amongst the newly grouped enclosed fields.

The husbandmen were the descendants of those medieval villagers who each had only a few acres and, as their land was insufficient for a living, often had a trade as well or worked casually for larger farmers. Those who lost their land through ill luck, debt, bad husbandry or the enclosures became landless labourers.

In the 16th and 17th centuries there is evidence that farm workers were mostly young, unmarried men who lived in the attic rooms of the farmhouse. During the late 17th and 18th centuries many small farms were amalgamated and the farmhouses this released were divided up into two or three labourers' cottages. They usually remained so divided until the present century.

Labourers' cottages built as such by a farmer or large estate were not a feature of the countryside until the late 18th and early 19th centuries. They were then sometimes given very decorative external features but were of extremely plain design inside. Frequently they were grouped or built in symmetrical pairs or short terraces. After the enclosure of outlying lands in the parish they might be built near where the cattle were pastured and where a field barn had been built so that the labourers were on hand to look after the animals.

The Geology of Wiltshire and Neighbouring Southwestern Counties

This map is reproduced from 'Houses in the Landscape' by kind permission of the authors, John and Jane Penoyre and the publishers Faber and Faber. It shows the broad band of oolitic limestone which forms the Cotswolds and continues down the West side of Wiltshire into East Somerset and Dorset with a further small tongue stretching into Southeast Wiltshire. Next to it is the area of greensand, an unsuitable building material, where timber buildings predominated until brick became available. To the East are the chalk downs, influenced by the building traditions of the chalk areas further East in other counties. There are also two small areas by the Eastern border of the county where suitable clays enabled timber buildings to be at a relatively early date supplemented by brick buildings.

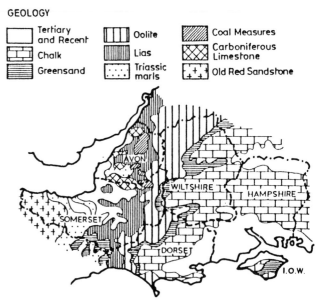

GEOLOGY

Tertiary and Recent — Chalk — Greensand — Oolite — Lias — Triassic marls — Coal Measures — Carboniferous Limestone — Old Red Sandstone

6

The Traditional Building Materials of Wiltshire

The divisions on this map are based on an analysis of surviving (listed) buildings dating from before 1840 made by Wiltshire County Council. Had such a map been made in 1600 the areas dominated by timber-framing would have been much more extensive reaching, for example, to Trowbridge, Chippenham and the Wylye valley near Warminster.

CRICKLADE

HIGHWORTH

MALMESBURY

STONE TILE some clay some slate
STONE some rendering

SWINDON

CHIPPENHAM

CALNE

AVEBURY

MARLBOROUGH

CORSHAM

THATCH CLAY TILE some slate
TIMBER-FRAME BRICK some stone some stucco

MELKSHAM

BRADFORD-ON-AVON

DEVIZES

PEWSEY

TROWBRIDGE

WESTBURY

THATCH CLAY TILE some slate
FLINT BRICK some stone some cob

WARMINSTER

AMESBURY

THATCH CLAY TILE some slate
STONE some brick some stucco

MERE

WILTON

SALISBURY
THATCH
CLAY TILE
TIMBER-FRAME
BRICK
some stucco

TISBURY

Building Materials

The nature of Wiltshire's traditional architecture is determined above all by the position of the county within England and by the properties of the building materials which were available close at hand. The county is situated astride the boundary between what archaeologists have called 'highland' and 'lowland' Britain. West of the boundary lies an area of stone building allied to the Cotswolds and to Somerset and Dorset. Roughly East of the line lie the clay valleys with their timber-framed buildings and the Downland areas with houses of cob, chalk blocks and flint.

In the area of the best limestone around Corsham, Box and Bradford-on-Avon the houses which survive from the 16th century have walls about 26" thick, of rubble construction. By the 17th century the usual thickness was 24" unless the house was especially tall. In the 18th century this lessened to about 22" and the stonework was increasingly brought to courses until in the second half of the century the stones were roughly squared. In the 19th century large blocks of fine ashlar (fully squared stone) became normal and the side wall thickness was reduced to 19" or less, the end walls often retaining greater thickness (even when they did not incorporate chimney stacks) to act as buttresses.

No. 1
Townsend Cottage, All Cannings, a former farmhouse dating from the late 16th century. The parlour end to the left protrudes slightly in front of the hall as a forward facing gable. It is not a true crosswing as the main roof is continuous. In the 18th century the parlour end framing was replaced by brick. This house like many of its type was later divided into cottages.

No. 2
Framing of the hall of Townsend Cottage showing the two main bays with ogee (wavy) bracing and the shorter smoke bay to the right where the house originally ended. The whole of the roof above the smoke bay is blackened with soot. In 1909 there was an entrance door through the two lower panels to the left. The building always had two storeys but the eyebrow dormer window is an 18th century addition.

Further North in the Biddestone area the stone was quarried from beds with narrow horizontal layers and more mortar had to be used between these tile-like stones. To protect the surface it was plastered over. In the Southwest of the county the stone from the Chilmark area was a good freestone which was commonly used in ashlar blocks even in the 17th century. In the Northeast of Wiltshire sarsen, an extremely hard stone, was available and was often used for the plinths of timber-framed buildings in unshaped boulders. Sections of sarsen rubble wall are found dating back as far as the 17th century in cottages in the Kennet valley but it could not be readily cut into squared blocks until power tools were introduced in the mid 19th century.

In the medieval period timber-framing had been reasonably common even in the limestone area but by the 16th century it was in very limited and usually ornamental use in the highland region. Stone and part stone wings were being added to good quality timber buildings in the transitional area around Trowbridge which was at that time very prosperous through the wool trade. In the valley between Trowbridge and Potterne in the early 17th century there was a fashion for buildings with stone ground floors and timber-framing above. In the 17th century, too, newly-built timber-framed houses in villages as far apart as Bremhill, Keevil and Stockton sometimes had end stack walls of stone.

The timber-framing of the 16th century was usually in fairly large panels with curved braces at the ends of the bays. The walls were often three panels high. At the end of the century ogee (wavy) braces became fashionable. In the 17th century panels were usually smaller and more regular and the braces were often straight. Some close studding was used in the 16th century but it was especially popular in the early 17th century (*see nos 9 and 10*). The use of timber-framing as an external material for houses seems to have died out in the county around 1720. Late examples have the minor timbers nailed instead of pegged and long diagonal braces were used (*see no. 16*). Stud walls clad in lath and plaster continued to be built in the Devizes area in the 18th century.

During the 17th century brick began to be used decoratively as nogging in the panels of timber-framed houses. It usually replaced earlier wattle and daub but in some cases seems to be original. It was usually laid in a herringbone pattern. By the

No. 3
Former farmhouse of the 16th century at East Coulston. The two panels at the left end reflect the timber-framed fireplace area in the hall, the next two panels span the rest of the hall. The thicker post supports the partition between the hall and the parlour, which is two panels long at the right end. Two of the braces have been removed for later windows.

second half of the 17th century it was also being used by estates for alterations to houses, and sometimes for the construction of ovens and chimneys. Though previously some gentry houses had been built of brick it was not until about 1700 that it came increasingly into use in the lowland area to replace or partly rebuild small timber-framed houses. The part of the county where this took place to the greatest extent was the Pewsey valley where, perhaps through a shortage of good wood but more likely because of the lack of additional wealth from the woollen trade, timber buildings were in general of poorer quality.

Brick was also used to dress the quoins and window and door openings of stone buildings, for example in the Highworth, Seend and Warminster areas, where the stone was not of the best quality.

No. 5
16th century stone farmhouse at Thingley, Corsham. The original house reaches from the left chimney to just right of the present front door. It had a hall to the left with end chimney and a small parlour. In the early 18th century the walls were raised in height, and the right hand part was added on. The evidence for all this lies in the roof and interior as the outside stonework was carefully matched. At the far left is a barn, attached in the 18th century. In the 19th century part of its ground floor was converted to a dairy, of which the door and window can be seen.

No. 4
Late 16th century house at Erlestoke. The top row of panels of the framing was added in the early 18th century, hence the house's unusual appearance. It has a lobby entrance plan with the hall to the right and the parlour to the left. The ground floor window positions are original.

From the 17th century, if not earlier, houses close to the chalk downs were built of mixed materials; stone or brick combined with the weaker materials, chalk or flint. In better houses the materials were used decoratively, in bands or chequers but in poorer houses the materials were intermixed or in patches. Cob was also used extensively in these areas but whole houses of cob are now found chiefly in the Southeast of the county where very little fieldwork has been carried out by the Wiltshire Buildings Record.

No. 6
Farmhouse of about 1600 at Holt on a site inhabited at least since Saxon times. This is the rear of the house which is seen from the present road which was constructed in the late 18th century. The house was built two full storeys high and with a useable attic. Its ground floor plan, however, remains the simple one of heated hall to the right and unheated parlour in a false crosswing to the left. The 'crosswing' chimney was added later blocking the three windows. The dormer in the roof is also later, the attic being originally lit only by windows in the forward and end gables. To the right, part of an added dairy with cheeseroom over can be seen.

Throughout the county almost all of the very poorest houses of previous centuries have gone but there is some documentary evidence of what they were like and fragments sometimes remain built into later replacements. A few complete examples have survived as outbuildings.

This flimsy evidence suggests that in the 17th century in the limestone area the poorest houses had stone walls much thinner than the better houses and bonded together with a soft mud mortar. In the timber-framed areas the posts of the poorer houses were not set up on plinths in the normal way but were put straight into the earth and were therefore likely to rot sooner. The timbers also were of poorer quality and of smaller section, with waney (unshaped) outside edges and less heart wood so they, too, lasted less long though the plan of the house might be similar to that of better houses.

Richard Jefferies writing in 1874 described a small single storey house which a labourer built for himself and his family on quit-rent land near Swindon. It had a thatched roof, a floor of hard mud and at least one wall of wattle and daub but was divided into a living room and another room so small you could reach across it.

House Plans

The layout of a building derives from local tradition and also reflects the wealth and status of the inhabitants. The plan types found in Wiltshire are all related to those found in surrounding counties and yet the county has its own distinctive characteristics. The highland/lowland division is certainly important and outside the limestone areas the whole of Wiltshire is in the transitional area which stretches into Berkshire and Oxfordshire where Southwestern plan types are quite frequently found but Eastern types predominate. The general tendency in the lowland area is for houses to be smaller than in the highland area with secondary functions like grain storage and brewing carried out in separate buildings.

The medieval three room and cross passage plan which persisted in Somerset and Dorset into the 17th century seems to have lost its hold earlier in highland Wiltshire. By the 16th century it was rarely used as a plan type for new buildings. The idea of having entry into a passage lingered on to some extent but often there was no door leading out of it at the back of the house.

No. 7
House of about 1600 at Horton, Bishops Cannings, photographed in 1983 before re-thatching. The front range has a lobby entrance plan with an additional service room. It has two large gable dormers. An unheated room in a rear wing is slightly later and may be a summer parlour or court room. The house has ogee bracing and is remarkable for its many oriel windows with variously decorated brackets (no. 8).

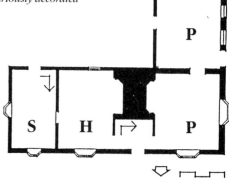

Plan 1 *The above house at Horton*

No. 8

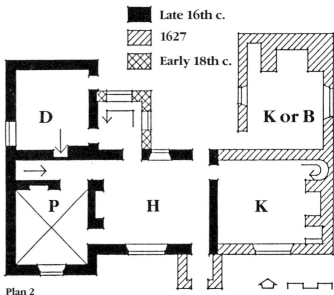

Late 16th c.

1627

Early 18th c.

Plan 2
Great Lypiatt Farm, Corsham

Some Wiltshire manor houses and large farmhouses apparently of the 16th or 17th centuries in the limestone belt have complicated plans, difficult to understand. This is usually the result of the phenomenon known as 'alternate rebuilding' in which only the oldest part is demolished when improvement is required. At the next modernisation a different part is pulled down and rebuilt. Great Lypiatt Farm, Corsham (*front cover and nos. 32, 70, 72 and 94*) may be an example of this process, the present building having replaced in a piecemeal fashion an earlier house on the site.

In the lowland area a two room plan of hall and parlour seems to have been standard from the medieval period onwards with, in the 16th century, the addition of one or two upper chambers. The hall was the main living room where cooking and eating took place and the parlour was used for sleeping and storage.

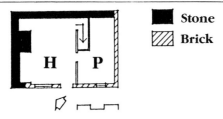

Stone

Brick

Plan 3
Chalk stone cottage at East Coulston (probably 17th century) with the front and end walls rebuilt in brick in 1774. The masonry next to the fireplace is sealed off but may hold an oven or curing chamber.

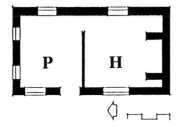

Plan 4
Early 18th century flint, stone and brick banded house at Hanging Langford in Steeple Langford parish.

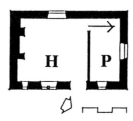

Plan 5
Late 17th or early 18th century stone house at Donhead St Andrew.

Larger houses had the parlour as a crosswing or had three rooms in an L plan.

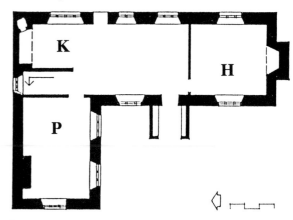

Plan 6
Early 17th century L plan stone manor house at Broughton Gifford. The kitchen probably extended into the present stair area and the centre of the house may have contained a staircase and buttery.

By the early 17th century there were also T plans with the kitchen as a wing behind the middle of the house.

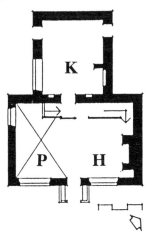

Plan 7
Early 18th century farmhouse with T plan at Bradford Leigh, South Wraxall. The main house is two storeys high and the single storey kitchen may have been the detached brewhouse of an earlier farmhouse.

The kitchen assumed greater importance at this period. There is some documentary evidence to suggest that in the 17th century where a house had only two ground floor rooms but both were originally heated, one room was the hall and the other the kitchen. The functions of the parlour were taken over by first floor rooms.

No. 9
Farmhouse of about 1600 at Langley Burrell Without, situated in a transitional area between the timber-framed and stone traditions. The framing is close studding, three sections tall, infilled with the local flat stones instead of wattle and daub. The windows including the roof dormer are 18th century casements, probably replacing wooden oriels. At each end of the front and rear walls is a length of stone walling and the end walls are stone. The ground floor plan comprises a simple hall with end stack and a parlour. The hall is to the right of the photograph. The lower roof beyond covers a dairy with cheeseroom above added in the 18th century (see no. 98).

The liking for wings shown in many of the plans was a feature of most of the county. The rear outshuts so favoured in Somerset, which might have been an alternative, are very little found except to some extent in Southwest Wiltshire.

15

No. 10
The Court House, Bratton. The main range to the left is basically a medieval cruck building. The jettied crosswing to the right was built on to it in the 16th century to replace the very small parlour and perhaps to provide a courtroom. The large forward-facing gable was added on to the front of the hall by John Whitaker, a clothier. Carved woodwork in the hall has his and his wife's initials and the date 1626. The house is a good example of ornamental timber-framing and there is herringbone brick nogging in the crosswing gable.

Some basically two-roomed village houses of the 17th century have a low or poorly built third room attached at either the hall or the parlour end. The suspicion that these were sometimes connected with a trade is confirmed in the case of a house at Avebury where documentary evidence shows it to have been a mercer's 'shop'. An unheated third room of this type seems in some cases to have been a dairy.

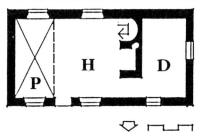

Plan 8
Stone farmhouse called the Milk House at Purton. The dairy was an extension and has a datestone 1656.

In lowly houses in the centre and East of the county there is some evidence of a tradition of an attached fuel shed like the 'hovels' of Oxfordshire. Examples of this are shown in nos. 23, 24 and 25.

The most obvious difference between the traditions of the highland and lowland areas is in the positioning of fireplaces. To the East when fireplaces were put into older open hall houses with three rooms and a cross passage in the 16th and 17th centuries they were usually put at the 'upper' or best end of the hall, backing on to the parlour. To the West they were put at the 'lower' or service end of the hall, backing on to the cross passage. These traditions seem to have led to the lobby entrance plan of the East with a massive stack in the middle of the house between hall and parlour and to the house plans with gable end stacks of the West.

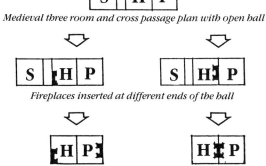

Medieval three room and cross passage plan with open hall

Fireplaces inserted at different ends of the hall

Two room plans with gable end or central stacks

No. 11
A former manor house at Wingfield which belonged to Keynsham Abbey until the Dissolution but from 1494 is known to have been leased and later owned by wealthy clothiers. This, like no. 10, was a medieval house to which the crosswing to the right and a dairy and cheeseroom wing behind were added in the late 16th century. In 1636 the addition of the two small forward wings and the central dormer gave the house its present appearance. The left wing contains a staircase as can be seen from the window position at mid height. The relieving arches over the windows added strength but were chiefly decorative. There is evidence from a drawing and from the tithe map of 1841 that the building once extended further to the left.

The houses shown in nos. 4, 14, 18 and 23 clearly illustrate the central stack tradition and nos. 5, 15, 17, 28 and the back cover are a few of the examples of the end stack tradition.

In Somerset and Dorset there is a common 17th century plan type known as the 'central service room' or 'unheated central room' plan. The central room was at the rear of the house opposite the front door and was used as a ground floor 'cellar' for beer or cider storage or as a dairy. It often housed the main stair. This plan is only occasionally found in Wiltshire (*no. 15*) and is sometimes even then an alteration from an earlier plan where, for example, a heated kitchen is added to the parlour end of a two roomed house with a heated hall and a small unheated parlour. The nearest equivalent to the plan is found in L shaped manor houses where the main entrance is into a staircase hall with a buttery behind (*see plan 6. No. 71 illustrates the buttery behind the staircase area at Rowden Farm, Lacock*).

Medium-sized newly built or rebuilt farmhouses of the beginning of the 18th century were still usually one room deep. Even so they were an improvement on their predecessors in that they had more fireplaces, higher rooms and, in the parlour, panelled walls and built-in cupboards. The usual height of the building had become two full storeys with additional attic space, and cellars became more common, normally being positioned under the parlour. Higher up the social scale in villages 'double pile' houses (two rooms deep) with hipped roofs became standard (*see no. 21*).

The lowliest houses of the 18th century remained usually only 1½ storeys high with one or two rooms on the ground floor. At the end of the century the estate cottages being built by fashionable landlords usually retained a simple traditional plan but often provided a back kitchen or wash-house.

No. 13
A house at Ogbourne St George with a flint and sarsen banded gable end probably replacing an earlier timber-framed wall as the range behind it is still largely framed.

No. 12
Elmbury Cottage, Wylye. Flint and stone are banded decoratively on the facade of this early 17th century house. The rear wall is much plainer. The original house was very simple, being just a heated hall, an unheated parlour and rooms over, partly in the roof. Later the leanto extension to the left, the windows in the thatch and the thatched porch were added.

No. 14
17th century farmhouse at Fovant with lobby entry plan. At the left end is an additional service room, perhaps a dairy. The windows and doors of the facade were later replaced but a plain chamfered mullioned window remains at the rear.

No. 15
Farmhouse of chalkstone at Compton Bassett, dating from the 17th century. This house has a central unheated room plan (see page 17). The hall is to the left, the stairs rise in the centre over a small room and the parlour is to the right.

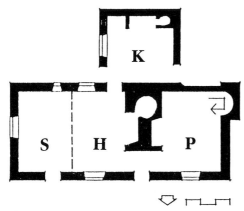

Plan 9 *The Firs, Fovant*

No. 16

South Cottage, Conock, Chirton, a house built at the end of the timber-framing tradition in the early 18th century. On the ground floor it has a heated hall with end stack (to the right) and an unheated parlour. Typical of the late framing are the tall panels, the long straight bracing and the original eyebrow dormers.

No. 17

Cottage at The Derry, Ashton Keynes. This simple stone cottage dating from the 18th century is only 1½ storeys high. The newel staircase is beside the stack and to the right of the entrance a partition of tongue and grooved boarding divides off a small room. The wooden window lintels are typical of the 18th century in Northwest Wiltshire.

No. 18

Rhotteridge Farm, Melksham Without, an isolated farmhouse in Melksham Forest which was a freehold in the 18th century. The land was enclosed in about 1611 and a stone house may have been built then, a portion of which remains to the right and in the footings. There are diary references to the owner Thomas Smith of Shaw visiting workmen there between 1716 and 1722 and this may be the date of the rebuilding in brick. It is a lobby entrance house with an additional room. The portion at the far left is an extension.

No. 19

Starveall Farm, Chippenham Without called New Farm on John Norris's estate map of 1728. It was probably built on a new site by John who lived at The Ivy, Chippenham or his father William of Nonsuch House, Bromham who had acquired the estate in 1711. A central passage divides the hall from the parlour. The kitchen is in a hipped wing to the rear (see no. 75). The main roof is hipped at both ends and the windows have ogee moulded mullions.

No. 20
Manor Farm, Conock, Chirton. A late 17th or early 18th century home farm for Conock manor built as a simple house with hipped roof and a stair turret at the rear but with wings added later behind. (Roof details, no. 97.)

No. 21
Gentleman's farmhouse at Whistley, Potterne. An impressive rebuilding of an older copyhold farmhouse which in 1719 had only a hall, a kitchen/ brewhouse, two passages, two little rooms, a buttery and a dairy on the ground floor. The copyhold was renewed in 1730 by Henry Kent and in 1765 the building was described as a 'fayre dwelling house'. Parts of the older house are incorporated at the rear.

No. 22

Late 18th century brick house at Great Cheverell, one room deep with a central staircase. The hall/kitchen is to the left and the parlour, to the right of the door, was originally unheated. The room's length to the far right is an extension. The roof is plain tiled. (Porch detail, no. 34)

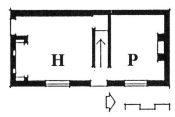

Plan 10 *House at Great Cheverell, above*

No. 23

Cottage at Kepnal, Pewsey. This was originally a timber-framed building, with a lobby entrance plan. It was largely rebuilt in brick, probably at the end of the 18th century, and the front part of the parlour end was turned into an outhouse or workshop. The rear part is a narrow room reached from a doorway beside the small stair behind the stack.

No. 25

Peartree Cottage at New Mill, Milton Lilbourne, like no. 24 above, is an example of poor quality building. It probably dates from the beginning of the 19th century and was demolished in 1981. It was almost square in plan and had a main heated living room on the ground floor with two small additional rooms behind the stack in a leanto. A lath and plaster partition divided the upper floor. The construction combined late timber-framing (at the gable ends and in the walls), limestone (perhaps brought from the Bradford-on-Avon area along the Kennet and Avon Canal), red bricks and yellow bricks (in places rendered), chalk rubble and cob. Many of the building materials were re-used and the stack may have remained from an earlier building on the site. Above one of the first floor windows is a hoist.

No. 24

Cottage at Peppercombe, Urchfont dated 1774 on a brick above the doorway. The front and rear walls are 16" thick and made of chalk rubble faced with brickwork on a sarsen and flint plinth. The house is 2½ storeys high and was formerly thatched. It has one large squarish living room on the ground floor (see no. 88) and a single storey outhouse attached, made largely of re-used timber-framing and with a solid thatch roof (not visible in picture). This is the only domestic example of solid thatch which the Buildings Record has found. Furze and twigs were piled on top of flat joists and the whole was thatched over in the ordinary way. Horizontal weatherboarding and, apparently, new wattle and daub were used to weatherproof the East gable of the main structure which was made out of a reused roof truss.

Windows

Very few 16th century windows survive in timber-framed houses. Where they do it is usually because the window has been hidden by a later extension or by cladding. The examples found show that they normally had plain diamond mullions (*like those of the grille in no. 41 but rather larger in section*) or were hollow moulded like stone mullioned windows of the period.

By the end of the 16th century in stone houses reserved chamfered mullions (*see page 27*) were sometimes used (front cover, section of the house to the left). At about the same time the first use of ovolo (quarter round) moulded mullions began (*no. 37 and also visible in 70*) and these were to continue in popularity during the whole of the 17th century. No. 8 shows a wooden ovolo moulded oriel window. Oriel windows were extremely popular in the early 17th century for those who could afford them and the pegholes for their brackets are often found when the windows themselves have been replaced (*no. 9 has such holes and no. 10 would probably have had oriels*).

In the 18th century stone mullions were still used, usually with ogee (S shaped) or bead mouldings. In the late 18th century plain squared mullions were preferred. Over much of the county casement windows with leaded lights became common for houses of middling quality (*nos. 9 and 15*) and

No. 26

An estate cottage at Roundway, possibly for a gamekeeper. This was a simple building with lobby entrance plan, constructed in the 18th century, partly (perhaps wholly), of stud walling with a lath and plaster outer covering. In the 19th century the house was extended to the rear and the roof was raised. The Gothic first floor windows, the carved pendants at the eaves and the ornamental rustic porch were added to make the building an attractive feature in the grounds of the estate. In 1984 the remains of kennels were visible in the rear garden. (Interior detail, no. 56 and plan 11)

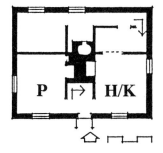

Plan 11 *Roundway.*

No. 27

Widbrook Farm, Bradford-on-Avon, a substantial farmhouse with a group of model farm buildings, built in 1834/5 for Earl Manvers' estate. It has a shallow pitched slate roof with overhanging eaves, ashlar stone walls and a rear wing with kitchen, brewhouse and dairy. (Details in nos. 43 and 104.)

No. 28

Brickyard Cottage, Ashton Keynes, probably dating from the 1830s. The main house is one room deep with an outshut at the back. It was constructed of bricks, perhaps manufactured at the site, which were covered with stucco incised to resemble ashlar stone. There was a range in the main living room to the left and a best fireplace in the parlour to the right.

No. 29

Pair of farmworkers' cottages at Temple Farm, Rockley, Ogbourne St Andrew, built probably in the mid 19th century and demolished in 1981. The walls were of worked sarsen stone with brick dressings. Sarsen, being so hard, could only be cut when machine tools became available around 1850. Temple Bottom was one of the main sources of the stone. No. 30 shows the rear view.

sashes began to appear on more pretentious houses with an urban flavour (*no. 21 shows segment-headed sashes and no. 27 shows early 19th century sashes with architrave surrounds*). At the end of the 18th century and in the early 19th century it was common for windows in brick walls to have slightly curved heads (*nos. 1, 22, 23, 25 and 29*).

No. 30

Porches

High quality stone and timber houses had been given porches since the medieval period but their use became more common on smaller manor houses and clothiers' houses from about 1600. An especially fine timber example, probably of 1626, is shown in no. 31 and one in stone dated the following year can be seen on the front cover and also in no. 32. Two storey porches, a considerable status symbol during the middle ages, might be found on the house of someone bordering between tradesman and gentleman in the early 18th century as shown in no. 33.

Flat canopies of wood or stone on brackets were very common in the Western and central parts of the county during the 18th and early 19th centuries. Examples are shown in nos. 14, 21, 34 and on the back cover. Early 19th century rustic porches can be seen in nos. 16 and 26 and an ironwork porch in no. 20. The enclosed ashlar porch of no. 19 is perhaps a 19th century addition and the enclosed porch with pointed arch of no. 28 is presumably original. The Urchfont cottage in no. 24 has a pentice roof on posts, added perhaps in the late 19th century, protecting the front door and the well pump.

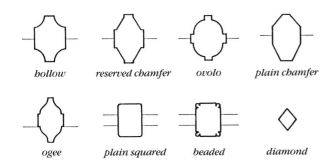

| hollow | reserved chamfer | ovolo | plain chamfer |

| ogee | plain squared | beaded | diamond |

Types of Mullion
'Outside' is towards the bottom of the page.
A single line indicates the glass and a double line a sub-frame.
Many minor variations in these types can occur.

No. 31
Timber-framed porch of about 1626 with foliage-carved arch and open balustrades on a flint and stone chequered plinth at the Court House, Bratton.

No. 32
Single storey porch of 1627 at Great Lypiatt Farm, Corsham, (see front cover) with foliage carved spandrels to the arch, early 18th century box sundial on the apex and datestone.

No. 33
Early 18th century two storey porch at Little Ashley, Winsley. Note the oval window, typical of the period, the beeboles (shelves for hives) in the angle and the string course rising for the lamp over the entrance.

Datestones and Inscriptions

Houses can sometimes be dated from documentary evidence but difficulties arise from the many which had no name apart from that of the current or previous tenant and were rebuilt many times on the same site. A surprising number of Wiltshire houses, however, have a date displayed or concealed somewhere on the fabric. Sometimes this commemorates the primary build but more often it refers to major alterations. Groups of three initials usually record a marriage but this was often also a time when work was done on the house. The surname initial is in the centre with the husband's initial to the left and the wife's to the right.

No. 34
Wooden canopy over the front door of the house at Great Cheverell shown in no. 22. This also shows the dentilled platband at first floor level.

No. 35
Datestone of 1584 (the 5 is upside down) on a house at Ashton Keynes. This was originally an outside wall.

Very few 16th century dates are found, most are of the 17th and 18th centuries with perhaps a tailing off in the 19th century. Favourite places for dates are over doorways, at the top of the facade, on chimneys, fireplace lintels, carved woodwork or on a tiebeam in the roof. Occasionally the date is scratched on a window pane or a coin is buried under the window sill. A range of types are shown in nos. 35, 36, 37, 38 and 39.

Numerous examples have been found of other objects being buried or hidden within a house at the time of building or alteration and this was no doubt done to bring good luck. Items found have included boots and shoes, glass bottles, iron tools and, more sinister, the walled-up remains of cats, rats, frogs and chickens.

No. 38
1773 inscribed on a brick at an Edington house.

No. 36
Damaged datestone of 1628 found at East Coulston.

No. 37
Datestone probably celebrating the marriage of Richard Maundrell and his wife H . . ., over an ovolo moulded mullioned window at a Compton Bassett manor house.

No. 39
R H 1784 inscribed on a floorboard at a Purton farmhouse, probably Richard Holliday or Halliday whose tombstone of 1836 is at the parish church.

Doors

In the 16th and 17th centuries the outer doors of the better houses were more strongly constructed than internal doors and often consisted of two layers of wood. They might, for example, be panelled on the outside and cross banded or diagonally strengthened with planks on the inside. Quite a number of these strong doors are still in use today. When plank doors were used, the joints might be protected from the weather by being covered with vertical strips (*see the privy door, for example, in no. 106*).

Good quality internal doors of the 17th century were often in six panels (*no. 40*) but during all the period covered by this book ordinary doors were made of battened planks; usually two or three wide planks in the 17th century (*no. 71*), increasing to three or four narrower planks in the 18th century (*nos. 73, 82 and 101*) and more in the 19th. Though much old ironwork survives, wooden latches are frequently seen (*no. 82*) and occasionally a half log to fit into iron holders to bar an outside door.

In the 19th century many older doors were removed from the ground floors of farmhouses and were replaced by smart new four-panelled doors (*no. 50*).

Rooms where food was stored such as butteries, dairies, cheeserooms, lofts and apple stores often had provision for ventilation. This might be an open grille at the top of a doorway or partition (*nos. 41, 44 and 80*), a partition of open work or even a lattice door (*nos. 42 and 43*).

No. 40
17th century panelled door with cocks head hinges in the attic of a former manor house at Hilperton. This door like many recorded has never been painted.

No. 41
Buttery doorway of the 17th century at Wingfield (see no. 11), hollowed out for the passage of barrels and ventilated and lit above by diamond mullions.

No. 42
Slatted door from the house at Hilperton (no. 40), probably 17th century. This door had been removed but is likely to have ventilated some sort of food store.

No. 43
Lattice door to an attic at Widbrook Farm, Bradford-on-Avon (see no. 27). There was a cheeseroom on the first floor and the attic may have been used for further cheese storage or as an apple store.

At all periods, when the occupant could afford it, external and internal doorways were chamfered or moulded in the taste of the day and usually matched the surrounds of any fireplaces of the same date in the building. No. 71 shows a moulded and stopped doorway.

Partitions and Beams

There is a considerable amount of fine carved woodwork dating from the late 16th century and the 17th century in the manor houses and good farmhouses of Wiltshire. The best examples are armorial overmantels, carved brackets supporting beams, carved bosses in panelled ceilings and carving associated with wall panelling (*no. 44*). There are also attractive spice cupboards (*no. 67*), sets of cupboards beside fireplaces and doors with applied carving. Not much of this is illustrated here as the aim of this book is to show the houses of a wide range of society and decoration was always associated with the wealthiest classes.

No. 44
Early 17th century partitioning with pierced top panels for light or ventilation at the Manor House, Box. Note the strapwork carving above. The panelling had been moved and may have been part of a lobby at the front door or a buttery within the hall.

Below the level of elaborate decoration, an even greater quantity of good quality woodwork is to be found of which the 16th century ceilings in nos. 45 and 46 are an example. The majority of beams, however, were not moulded but were chamfered. In the 16th and early 17th centuries the chamfers were usually quite wide, 3″–5″. The stops at the end of the chamfering were usually very simple (*no. 47*) but soon developed into a variety of forms (*nos. 48 and 50 for example*), some local and some used widely throughout England. Some of the most elaborate stops probably date from late in the 17th century.

No. 46
Panelled ceiling with moulded beams on wall posts moulded to match, in a 16th century farmhouse, Edington.

No. 45
16th century hall ceiling with moulded beam and chamfered and stopped joists at Purton.

Beams were of less importance in the 18th century and in the best houses were often hidden above plastered ceilings, (in the previous century there had been less decorative

plasterwork in Wiltshire than in some neighbouring counties). In large farmhouses beams were often still exposed and were large timbers with fairly wide chamfers and no stops. In general, however, chamfers became smaller during the 18th century because of the declining quality of the timber available.

In Wiltshire, after the medieval period, there was no tradition of a fine screen inside the main entrance door as there often was, for example, in Somerset. This was partly due to the disappearance of the cross passage and partly because where it existed the hall stack often backed on to it. However, there were sometimes good quality partitions of plank and muntin or staggered boards (bratticing) at the upper end of the hall (*no. 49*) or between the two upper chambers of a crosswing. A certain amount of 17th and 18th century panelling also survives, especially in parlours.

There were some stone houses with timber-framed partitions but at the lower end of the social scale partitions were usually made of the same material as the main walls of the house or, if they were not structural, of lath and plaster or occasionally reed and plaster. In the early 19th century vertical tongued and grooved boarding was often used.

No. 48
Three-sided double step and concave stop on an adzed beam of the early 17th century. Manor house at Easterton.

No. 47
Widely chamfered beam with simple stop supported by a wallpost set in a stone wall in a farmhouse at Langley Burrell Without, about 1600 (no. 9).

No. 49
16th century plank and muntin partition between the hall and parlour at the farmhouse, Thingley, Corsham (no. 5). Lath and plaster attached to it at a later date to make a smooth wall surface and now removed has caused the striped effect.

Fireplaces

In the early 16th century only a small number of superior houses had fireplaces as we know them today. The main living room, the hall, seems usually to have been open to the roof and its timbers are smoke-blackened (*no. 92*). The parlour was sometimes floored over to give a room above and sometimes not. During the century newly built houses were increasingly provided with either a smoke bay at the end of the hall or a timber-framed fireplace and smoke hood with all the panels filled with wattle and daub (*nos. 1, 2 and 3 for exterior views and nos. 50, 51, 92 and 93*). Evidence for this stage of fireplace development is fairly often seen in timber-framed houses but is less often detected in stone houses though a few examples have been found.

No. 50
Formerly timber-framed fireplace of around 1600 at Marston. The sides of the fireplace were later rebuilt in stone and a brick oven was constructed behind. Note the beam stop, top left.

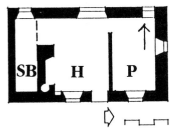

Plan 12
Early 16th century stone house at Purton built by the church authorities. A fireplace was later inserted in front of the hall's smoke bay, leaving it as a small room.

By the end of the 16th century kitchen fireplaces usually had stone jambs but the lintel was often a huge beam running right across the room and over openings to ovens, a staircase or a malt or bacon-smoking kiln at each side. This was probably a development from the smoke-bay beam. This type of fireplace was still being constructed in the early 17th century and at the same period there was another fashion for very deep fireplaces, probably also derived from the smoke

No. 51
A rear view of the timber-framed fireplace shown in no. 50, at first floor level. All the panels would have originally been infilled with wattle and daub.

No. 52
Kitchen fireplace of the 16th or early 17th century at a former manor house in Box parish.

bay. Some of up to 7' 9" depth have been recorded. In the stone area of Northwest Wiltshire a few segmental-arched kitchen fireplaces have been found (*no. 52*).

Kitchen fireplaces were nearly always associated with ovens and a variety of other features *(see page 42)* . In two-roomed houses the hall fireplace combined the functions for hall and kitchen. Where it did not need to, it often still had a small seat at one or both sides, of wood or stone and sometimes with an elbow rest. There might also be one or two small recesses in the back or side wall of the fireplace for keeping salt or tinder,

or for setting a candle (*no. 53*). Burn marks from rush lights suspended from the fireplace lintel are often seen, as are pegholes from wooden mantel shelves now gone and the fixing marks of former spit jacks and settles. Settles (*no. 85*) are rarely found still in their original position. They were usually fixed on to the side of the fireplace furthest out in the room and shielded the sitters from the draught of doors.

Parlour and chamber (i.e. first floor) fireplaces were normally slightly smaller and had none of these extra features (*nos. 54, 55, 56 and 57*). In the early 18th century parlour fireplaces of

No. 53
Stone fireplace with external stack in the hall of a timber-framed farmhouse at Poulshot. The fireplace may have been added to an open hall. This is a copy of an old photograph. The two curved alcoves in the back wall have now gone.

No. 54
Stone fireplace with chamfered and stopped surround and timber lintel in the chamber over the parlour at Horton, Bishops Cannings (see no. 7).

brick sometimes had curved side walls and by the end of the century the brick arches of cooking fireplaces were usually supported by a strip of iron (*no. 58*). At this time rods often ran across up inside the chimney on which a notched "pot hangell" of iron could be hooked (*just visible in no. 86*) or there was a hinged chimney crane which swivelled out from the side wall (*no. 87*).

In the early 19th century the cast iron hob grate became normal in cooking fireplaces and appeared in a smaller version in bedrooms (*no. 59*). Once the large downhearth fireplace had evolved in the 17th century few major changes to it took place until the availability of coal led to the development of the hob grate and then the range.

No. 55
Stone fireplace with moulded surround and cornice in the chamber over the kitchen at a former manor house, Yatton Keynell. The iron fireback shows Adam and Eve in the Garden and has the initials of the early 17th century owner of the house.

No. 56
18th century parlour fireplace with a gun cupboard adjoining it, at Roundway (see no. 26).

No. 57
Early 18th century fireplace with bolection moulded surround and cornice at the Manor House, Broughton Gifford.

No. 58
Late 18th century brick fireplace with the arch supported on an iron band. House in a terrace of workers' cottages in Maiden Bradley with Yarnfield parish.

No. 59
Brick first floor fireplace, probably of the 18th century with a 19th century hob grate in South Cottage, Conock, Chirton (no. 16).

Bread Ovens and other Fireplace Features

Bread ovens were made of stone in the 16th century (*no. 60*) and also for most of the 17th century when they were often set inside of a tall, tapering recess with a flat top (*see no. 61*). In the 18th century they were built of brick and varied in size and shape, some being almost round and some elongated. The ovens had solid wooden doors which pushed into position and a few of these still survive (*no. 62*). In Wiltshire, as in Gloucestershire, such doors may have been smeared with clay on the inside to make them fireproof. The outer recess around the oven opening was smaller than it had been in the earlier period.

In the 19th century ovens were still made of brick with the bricks sometimes set on end to form the side walls (*no. 64*) a practice which may have begun in the preceding century. The door and door frame were now of cast iron. The door often had a decorative motif on it and its size was indicated by a number on the inside.

The opening into the oven was usually inside the hearth on the side or back wall of the fireplace (*no. 50*) or in the corner (*no. 63*). Faggots of wood were burnt inside the oven itself until the walls and floor were hot enough to cook the bread. Before baking, the cinders were raked out and the oven was wiped clean. In the 19th century some ovens were constructed outside of the hearth with a separate fireplace beneath (*no. 86*).

No. 60
Stone oven in the side wall of the kitchen fireplace. Manor House, Cloatley, Hankerton, probably about 1594.

No. 62
Wooden oven door, probably 18th century, in a cottage at Chilton Foliat.

No. 61
Brick oven built inside a 17th century stone opening in a farmhouse at Semington.

The oven was usually incorporated inside the masonry of the chimney stack but sometimes it caused a bulge in the outside wall or an oblong or rounded, roofed projection was built on the end or side of the house (*nos. 65 and 66*). This was a convenient method to use when a very large oven was needed or when an oven was being added. The most complete examples of external ovens have been found in the area of stone building on the West side of Wiltshire. So far only the foundations or scars of external brick ovens have been recorded in central and East Wiltshire. Ovens as a whole were certainly being built until the middle of the 19th century when home-baking was increasingly replaced by the village baker but some continued in use until this century.

No. 64
19th century oven lined with bricks set on edge and with a cast-iron door in a cottage at Milton, East Knoyle.

No. 63
A brick oven with cast-iron door in an older opening and an alcove with iron door to a gridded area in the hall fireplace of a farmhouse at Bratton.

There is a great deal of evidence that bacon joints were cured by smoking in Wiltshire either by hanging on ropes from hooks far up the chimney or in special curing chambers inside or adjoining the fireplace. The earliest and largest examples of such chambers which have been found have dated from the early 17th century. Sometimes the chamber is at ground floor level and sometimes on the first floor. The most complete examples seen have had walls encrusted with soot and hooks in the ceiling, as was found in no. 86. Smoke may enter the chamber via a flue from the fireplace or can be funnelled into it by a flat sloping hood of stone inside the fireplace. There must then be a return flue from the top of the chamber back into the main chimney.

No. 65
18th century external oven at Westwood.

No. 66
Roofed external oven behind a brewhouse fireplace lit by a small fire window, in the farmhouse at Easton, Corsham. The brewhouse wing was added in the 17th or 18th century.

Fireside chambers may sometimes also have been used for the malting which was the first stage of home brewing. Traces of grain may be found and a ledge several feet up the chamber on which a hurdle was laid with a hair cloth on it holding the grain being malted. Unfortunately curing or malting chambers have often been taken for priest's holes (much rarer features) when discovered and have not been properly examined before conversion into useful cupboards.

Cupboards

Recesses associated with fireplaces have already been mentioned and there are sometimes also open recesses in the walls beside staircases, most probably for a candle. Small closed, and frequently lockable, wall cupboards were especially a feature of the 17th century (*no. 67*). It is usually assumed that they were for spices but there are sometimes a number of such cupboards in a good quality manor house and in the bedchambers they could well have been used to store money, jewellery and important documents.

No. 67
Carved 17th century spice cupboard in the hall of a farmhouse on the edge of East Kennett in West Overton parish.

The majority of small 17th century cupboards are fairly plain with only a little moulding around the door but they often have attractive butterfly hinges. 18th century cupboards are usually larger, are more often grouped (*no. 56*) and usually have H or HL shaped hinges. Next to the parlour fireplace at this time, even in fairly small houses, there was very often a tall semi-circular cupboard with shaped shelves and perhaps a shell top.

The doors to the more utilitarian kinds of wall cupboards are less likely to survive and this makes no. 68 particularly interesting.

No. 68
Plain 18th century cellar cupboard with double doors, Chapel Farm, Blunsdon St. Andrew.

Staircases

The position of the stair in a 16th century house can often be identified by a break in the pattern of the joists but the original stair itself does not usually survive. Around 1600 manor houses sometimes had newel stairs made with solid wooden treads (*no. 69*) or of solid blocks of stone. It was common for a stair to be either in a turret or in the area beside a chimney stack (*no. 70*). If the stair has been moved to the centre of the building in the 18th or 19th century, a curved wall may be the only evidence for its original position. Another clue sometimes is a small stair window especially if it is at mid height between floors.

A newel stair needed no balusters beside it, occupied a ground floor area only about 3ft. square and pivoted round a post of circular, square or octagonal section. The space underneath it where the top part swung round was utilised usually for a cupboard, an oven, a doorway (*no. 50*) or even (*in no. 88*) a copper.

If the staircase rose from the hall or the kitchen warm air was likely to escape from the room and there was usually a door at the foot of the stair to prevent this.

In the 17th and 18th centuries, in houses where the space and the timber could be afforded, an open well staircase was preferred (*nos. 71 and 72*). The best balusters were turned (*nos. 70 and 71*). A cheaper method was to saw splat balusters out of a plank (*dog gate at the foot of the stair in no. 71*). At the end of the 17th century there was a fashion in

No. 69
Newel stair of about 1594 with solid oak treads in a stair turret to the rear of the hall in the Manor House at Cloatley, Hankerton.

No. 70
Newel stair of 1627 which rises next to the hall fireplace showing the turned balustrade on the first floor at Great Lypiatt Farm, Corsham (front cover and no. 72).

furniture and staircases for twisted balusters which continued into the early 18th century (*no. 72*).

During the 18th century turned balusters remained popular becoming very slender but in the early 19th century there was a desire for even greater simplicity and plainness of style and stick balusters came into use.

No. 73
Top of the newel stair to the main attic and plank door to the attic over the dairy wing in a farmhouse, Langley Burrell Without (see no. 9).

No. 71
Staircase arch, staircase and buttery door, probably late 17th century, from the entrance passage at Rowden Farm, Lacock, a building of manorial status.

No. 72
Early 18th century staircase with twisted balusters in an added stair turret at Great Lypiatt Farm, Corsham (front cover and no. 70).

Dairies and Cheeserooms

Dairying activities in the 16th and early 17th centuries were usually on a small scale and may have been carried out in the kitchen of three-roomed houses and the hall of those with two rooms. However, in manor house inventories there are usually references to the white house (dairy) and the chamber over the white house containing cheese, showing that separate rooms were already provided. Where the third room of a small farmhouse is suspected to be a dairy the only distinguishing feature may be a lack of windows, especially on the South side.

During the 17th century dairying became increasingly important. In the 18th century when it had become a major industry in the county, dairy outshuts were sometimes built on behind existing houses (*no. 75*) or the dairy was accommodated in either a rear wing (*no. 20*), an extension in line with the main house (*nos. 6 and 9*) or a rear room of a double pile house with the cheeseroom above it. Outside the dairy there was usually an open-sided leanto where milk could be brought and left under cover (*nos. 74, 75 and 77*). Dairy doors are often four feet wide so that the pails could be brought in hanging on a yoke (*no. 85*). The windows normally had shutters or louvres instead of glass (*no. 76*) and the dairy interior was furnished with working tops, a few shelves, a cheese bench and cheese vats (*nos. 78, 79, 80 and 81*). By the mid 19th century some farmhouses in the cheese producing areas even had two dairies. Detached dairies are less common and being farm buildings in their own right are not included in this book.

No. 74
Pentice (leanto) roof on ornate stone pillars outside a dairy and brewhouse. Farmhouse at Easton, Corsham (see no. 66 for the other side of the wing).

It is clear that cheese storage was frequently in the attics of the farmhouse when there was no special cheeseroom. Evidence for this lies in named attic doors (*no. 82*) and in the remains of cheese racks which can still sometimes be seen.

When the cheeseroom was directly over the dairy it was usually reached by a special narrow wooden stair, with a balustrade and handrail in the room above (*no. 83*). The cheeseroom was fitted with rack and tack – moveable planks (the tack) which rested on the arms of the rack (*nos. 83 and 84*). The racks were along the walls or in rows in the middle of the room fixed to ceiling beams or joists. There was sometimes a hatch in the floor and a hoist for raising the cheeses.

No. 76
18th century cheeseroom window at the Manor House, Cloatley, Hankerton. The two outer lights are louvred and the two central ones have leaded panes.

No. 75
Simple pentice with wooden posts on padstones infilling the area next to the rear kitchen wing at Starveall Farm, Chippenham Without (see no.19).

No. 77
Dairy and cider house range of 1816 at a farmhouse in Lacock parish. The dairy is at the left end with a pentice roof over the door, the central door leads to what was probably a taproom and the cider house is to the right with a half loft over, a cider press and a fireplace in the gable wall. There was formerly another pentice along the building. This is the only purpose-built cider house which the Wiltshire Buildings Record has recorded, since beer was the usual drink in the county.

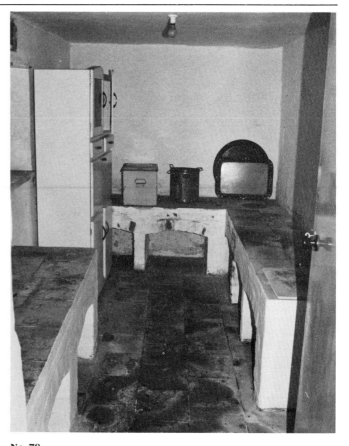

No. 78
Working tops and paved floor in a dairy at a manor house at Axford, Ramsbury.

No. 79
Lead lined wooden cheese vat and dairy shelf in the dairy shown in no. 77.

No. 80
19th century slate cheese vats and dairy shelf at the Manor House, Cloatley, Hankerton. Note also the paved floor with runnels and the remains of slatted ventilation to a storage area (and also over the door).

No. 81
Cheese bench used to support a meat safe in a corner of the dairy shown in no. 80.

No. 82
Plank door with wooden latch leading to an attic cheeseroom labelled to conform to the law of 1796. This allowed exemption from the window tax for cheeseroom windows. They had to be without glass and the word 'dairy' or 'cheeseroom' had to be painted on the door in black Roman letters at least 2" high. Here the signwriter seems to have cut his board too small. The room had to be used exclusively for dairying and could not be used as a bedroom. Chapel Farm, Blunsdon St. Andrew.

No. 83
Remains of 18th century cheese racks in the first floor cheeseroom at the Holt farmhouse (no. 6). The steep stair rises from the dairy in the far corner.

No. 84
Cheese racks, probably of 1816, with one of the loose shelves still in position, in the first floor cheeseroom of the range shown in no. 77. The posts for further racks, now gone, can be seen around the walls and the room has a fireplace.

No. 85
Stone paved dairy with open ladder to the cheeseroom at an Erlestoke farmhouse. With changing fashions the settle was moved out of the kitchen to the dairy. On it hangs a yoke for carrying pails of milk and beside it are two three-legged milking stools.

Few dairies are now used for their original purpose. They have usually been converted to alternative uses, often a kitchen or utility room. The furniture and fittings only survive when the dairy or cheeseroom has remained simply a storeroom.

Brewhouses

The brewhouse was usually less closely attached to the farmhouse than the dairy and cheeseroom and if it was not in a detached building it was usually to be found at the far end of the dairy range (*no. 66*). The plan below shows an unusually closely attached example, probably because the house had no kitchen. The brewhouse was usually used for baking as well as brewing and often also for washing clothes.

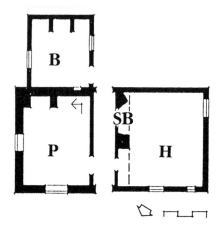

Plan 13
18th century single storey brewhouse built behind a 16th century timber-framed farmhouse with smoke bay at Marston. The parlour crosswing was rebuilt in the early 17th century with a stone ground floor, timber-framed above. Around 1900 a dairy was added behind the hall.

Most brewhouses were spacious, at least as large as the kitchen, where there was one, and they were often open to the rafters (*no. 86*).

No. 86
Brewhouse with fittings added later in about 1800 at Broadchalke. The building has an open fireplace with associated copper, oven, and curing chamber. The chamber is a cupboard of lath and plaster high up at the side of the stack with hooks in the ceiling. It is reached by ladder. Smoke was probably funnelled into it from the stack, returning through a flue.

No. 87
Brewhouse hearth of about 1800 at a farmhouse in Compton Bassett, showing the raised semi-circle of stones around the main cooking area. The iron chimney crane is hinged to pivot over the hearth, suspending cooking pots in the desired position. Although not visible in the picture, to one side of this fireplace is a copper and to the other an oven.

Like the floor of the dairy, that of the brewhouse was usually paved and there was normally a well pump inside the room (*no. 89*) or immediately outside (*no. 90*). No. 91 shows a domestic well with winding gear. Even in the 19th century the fireplace often remained open without a grate, so brewhouses are useful places to observe downhearths (*no. 87*).

No. 88
Copper probably added in the 19th century next to the cooking fireplace and under the stairs in the single living room at the cottage in Peppercombe, Urchfont shown in no. 24. A fire was lit under the copper to heat the water for washing and a flue leads into the main chimney. All the woodwork in the room, including the lid of the copper, is unpainted.

No. 89
The well pump and stone trough by the entrance to the brewhouse shown in no. 86. Note the stone paved floor.

No. 90
Well pump at the back of a house at Whitley, Melksham Without, where malting took place.

Roofs

R oofs are one of the most useful features of a house for dating purposes. They are out of sight and not subject to change for fashionable reasons. Good quality roofs have therefore often survived as a whole or in part in buildings which have been refronted or extensively altered on lower floors.

No. 92
Remains of a lath and plaster firehood of the 16th century inside the smoke-blackened hurdle roof of the hall at Robin Cottage, Tisbury. An outside doorway suggests that this small stone house, two bays long, was built around 1500. Hurdles were sometimes used as an alternative to riven laths as a basis for thatch. The semi-circle of blackened timber is part of an original smoke louvre which was plastered over when the firehood was inserted. In the 17th century the hood in turn was replaced by a stone fireplace and stack, just visible to the right.

No. 91
Stone well with partly collapsed superstructure behind a cottage of about 1500 at Potterne.

The two main types of roof are those with conventional trusses and those with crucks, which are curved timbers reaching from the foot of the walls or part way up the walls to the apex of the roof. Crucks were widely distributed in Wiltshire during the medieval period but since no cruck houses can be certainly dated to later than 1500, none have been illustrated in this book. In timber-framed buildings crucks were superseded by post and truss construction.

In the early 16th century collar and tiebeam trusses were probably the most common type of roof. At the apex where the two principal rafters meet, the joint at this time was usually a simple mortice and tenon. If a ridge piece was used it was often threaded through the uppermost principal, (*see no. 93*).

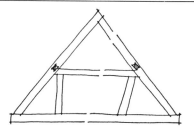

Fig. 2
Types of queen strut

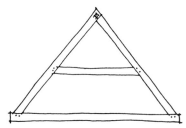

Fig. 1
Collar and tiebeam truss with threaded ridge piece

This method continued in common use until the early 17th century and occasional later examples are found.

Trusses with either vertical or raking queen struts were very common in Wiltshire in the 16th and 17th centuries. In the 16th century the collar and tiebeam were likely to be cambered.

No. 93
Early 16th century roof in a wing of Stowford Manor, Wingfield. The roof is windbraced throughout and the trusses have cranked collars and tenoned purlins. The apex joint is a typical one of the period. The end truss is filled with wattle and daub and was converted into a smoke bay, probably later in the 16th century.

King post roofs of the 16th century have been recorded in several buildings in Lacock and a few isolated examples of the 17th century have been found across the county. In the 18th century in Wiltshire, as in other counties, they gradually developed into one of the most common roof types of all, a position they continued to hold in the 19th century (*see no. 102*). Early examples were pegged and might be decorated with chamfering. In the 19th century it became normal to join the post to the tiebeam with an iron bolt.

Before the late 16th century the upper floors of many houses were open to the roof. This is shown by continuous plastering on the inside of end walls and partitions from first floor level upwards. In taller houses an attic floor was often inserted after the house was built giving in effect another storey. New stone houses of around 1600 were built with floored lofts and various ways were found to give more headroom to people moving amongst the roof timbers. Lofts were used for sleeping, for storing grain and other produce and at some manor houses for keeping pigeons (hence the term 'cockloft' for the roof space).

The adoption of dormer windows to light the newly created floored roof spaces was a natural development. When the house faced South or Southeast, as country houses usually did, dormers provided more and better light than the usual alternative of a small window at the gable end which might have to be fitted in next to a stack.

No. 94
Roof arrangement inside the late 16th century gable dormer at Great Lypiatt Farm, Corsham (see page 13 and front cover).

Dormers vary a lot in shape and size and the origin of the very large ones may lie in a process which began in the medieval period. It was then quite common for good quality houses in Wiltshire to have crosswings and from the front the gable of the crosswing was an imposing feature. At the end of the 16th century large gable dormers were built which imitated crosswings though they differed structurally. They were roofed in with the main house with a small extension roof to cover the dormer (*see nos. 1 and 6*). At about the same period houses were being built with one or more of these large gable dormers decorating the main front of the building and no longer in a crosswing position (*see front cover and nos. 7 and 10*).

When the process was still experimental the roof truss was sometimes awkwardly positioned partly across the area of the dormer (*no. 94*). This problem was overcome in the 17th century by altering the level of the purlins in front of the dormer and positioning the trusses themselves at the sides of the dormers. It was easier to do this if the dormers were smaller and this may partly explain why they became so at a later date (*see no. 11, in the centre*).

In the early 17th century as another method of making the attic more like a room, some houses were built with the floor of the roof resting on beams a couple of feet below the tops of the walls, the roof truss had no tiebeam and the collar was set at a rather lower than usual level. It could be braced in various ways.

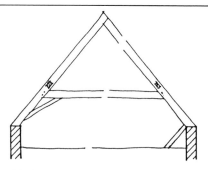

Fig. 3
Truss with low collar

In Gloucestershire there was a related solution for coping with the dormer problem. Huge beams called extended collars stretched across the roof taking the place of fully framed roof trusses and with purlins merely resting on top of them or principal rafters jointed into the top face on one or both sides. The advantage of this was that the extended collars rested on the lintels over the dormer windows and there were no feet of principal rafters to obstruct them. Variations in the extended collar system could be made depending on whether there were dormers on both sides of the roof, a wing or a stack behind the house and so on. The system could even be used to support the floor of the roof where it was on a level with the tops of the dormers. The use of extended collars has been recorded occasionally in Northwest, North and central Wiltshire on the fringe of the main area of their use, (*no. 97 shows an example in central Wiltshire*). Examples have varied greatly in their details and have dated from the early 17th century to the early 18th century.

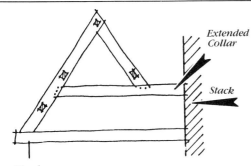

Fig. 4a
Composite extended collar truss

Extended Collar

Stack

No. 95
Original roof of a timber-framed late 17th century cottage at St Edith's Marsh, Bromham inside of the later, higher roof. It is a lobby entry house with an additional service room and this truss, closed with wattle and daub, divided the hall from the service end.

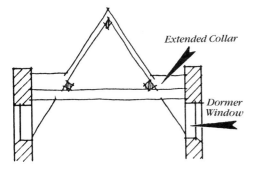

Extended Collar

Dormer Window

Fig. 4b
Extended collar truss without principal rafters

Another roof type found in Wiltshire during the 17th century was the truncated tiebeam truss, used chiefly but not exclusively in timber-framed houses. Its purpose was to provide a doorway through the roof truss from one first floor room to another in houses which were 1½ storeys high (*no. 96*). Sometimes earlier collar and tiebeam trusses were altered to this type when a fireplace was constructed and an upper floor inserted.

No. 96

The truss shown in no. 95 at first floor level. Note the tiebeam is interrupted to accommodate an original doorway between the bedchambers. Some wattle with the daub removed is exposed at the top of the wall but most of the wattle and daub has been replaced by brick nogging and the doorway has been blocked. Fig. 5 on page 65 shows the structure of the whole truss.

No. 97

Composite extended collar truss of about 1700 at Manor Farm, Conock, Chirton (see no. 20). This complicated arrangement allows the purlins running East/West at the rear of the roof to remain in line while the extended collar continues out to the stack wall supporting the rafters running North to the stack (see in Fig. 4a, page 63). Note also that the purlins are cut back where they are tenoned into the principal rafter (resting on the extended collar) and that at the far left a plank-like rafter forms the corner of the hip. There is also a conventional hip truss at right angles to the extended collar truss (not in view).

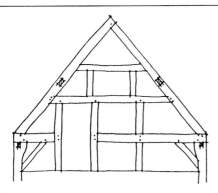

Fig. 5a
Interrupted tiebeam truss with two collars, at first floor level

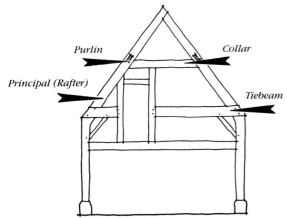

Purlin   Collar

Principal (Rafter)

Tiebeam

Fig. 5b
Interrupted tiebeam truss with single collar

At the end of the 17th century and the beginning of the 18th century the fashion for hipped roofs led to further changes in roofing methods. Sometimes the principal rafters of the hipped end were set at a slope on dragon ties (horizontal timbers across the corner of the building), sometimes there was also a hip rafter at the centre of the end wall, either straight or a knee principal, curved like a cruck (*see no. 99*). Knee principals were also used occasionally at this period where there were overhanging eaves and the feet of the common rafters needed to extend beyond the wall of the house.

No. 98
18th century roof over the dairy range at the farmhouse at Langley Burrell Without shown in no. 9. Some timbers are re-used but the side-lapped (rather than tenoned) collar, the long diagonal braces bisecting the rafters and the plated yoke at the apex can be seen.

Half hips were increasingly common on humbler buildings in the 18th century, especially where thatch was used, (*nos. 13, 17, 18, 23, 25, 26*). Sometimes older gable ends were altered to half hips.

Simple tenoned apex joints have already been mentioned. Some other apex types found in Wiltshire with their approximate dates are worth illustrating as in some cases they are one of the few dateable details in a roof.

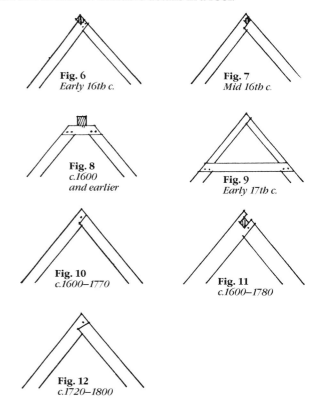

No. 99
Knee rafter used as a hip truss at Chapel Farm, Blunsdon St Andrew, early 18th century. (Other details seen in nos. 68 and 82).

Fig. 6
Early 16th c.

Fig. 7
Mid 16th c.

Fig. 8
*c.1600
and earlier*

Fig. 9
Early 17th c.

Fig. 10
c.1600–1770

Fig. 11
c.1600–1780

Fig. 12
c.1720–1800

A feature which divides the county is the use of a ridge piece in the roof. This square sectioned piece of timber supporting the tops of the rafters all along the roof was normal in the West but usually absent on the East side of the county. Related perhaps to this is the tendency to have clasped purlins on the East side of Wiltshire and usually tenoned purlins on the West (*no. 93 is a clear example of the latter*).

A plated yoke was often attached to the principal rafters at the apex in the 18th century as an additional support for the ridge piece and this can sometimes hide the apex joint, (*no. 98*). In the 19th century the ridge piece degenerated to a simple board, (*top of picture no. 102*), a process which may have begun at the end of the 18th century on occasions when suitable timber was not available.

Another important part of the roof truss was the collar. In the early 16th century these were often cambered for decorative reasons, (*no. 93*). Later they became flat (*nos. 95 and 98*) but narrow cambered collars are found again in the 18th century merely to provide more headroom (*no. 101*). It was quite common in the 17th century to use two or even three collars in a truss but in the 18th century the collar was sometimes omitted altogether and there was a tiebeam truss, a simple triangle with only one row of purlins each side of the roof. The way the collar was attached to the truss could vary. The tenoned collars of the 16th and 17th centuries (*nos. 93 and 96*) gave way to collars notch lapped on to the sides of the principal rafters in the 18th century (*no. 98*). It was quite common to make use of this technique to improve headroom as an existing tenoned collar could be removed and a lapped collar added instead at a higher level without disturbing the whole truss.

No. 100
Attic floor at Vine Cottage, Charlton (St Peter). This is an old form of construction in which round pieces of timber like rungs are sprung into holes in the sides of the joists providing staves for a wattle and daub floor. Similar holes in joists have been found elsewhere in Wiltshire and in other counties but here a large part of the floor survives intact. Such a floor may have been quite strong when new but becomes very brittle with age. To the left the old floor has been replaced by lath and plaster, in the centre the 'ladder' construction is visible with later lath and plaster below it. To the right even the old surface of the daub remains. This thatched roof dates from 1798 (or perhaps 1748) the date on the front of the building. It has a mixture of pole rafters (seen here), and sawn rafters. One piece of hurdling (a later example of the type shown in no. 92) was used under the thatch.

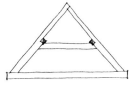

Fig. 13
Clasped purlins with diminished principals

No. 101
Roof truss of about 1784 (see no. 39) at Purton with a cambered collar and infilled with vertical boarding and a plank door to divide the roof space into rooms.

No. 102
19th century king post roof in a farmhouse at Whaddon, Semington.

Purlins along the sides of the roof between trusses were a standard feature of Wiltshire roofs in the whole of the period covered by this book. In the 16th century to the West of the county they were usually tenoned into the principal rafters and at that time normally strengthened by curved windbraces (*no. 93*). Straight windbraces were still sometimes used in sections of a roof until the early 18th century but their regular use was declining by the early 17th century. In the 18th century they were sometimes replaced by long diagonal braces bissecting the comon rafters (*no. 98*). There were small differences in the way purlins were tenoned. They often had soffit spurs in the 17th century, overlapped at the joint in the early 18th century, and during the century it became increasingly common to cut them back at the principal rafters (*no. 97 shows an early example*). Around 1800 they were frequently tusk tenoned (*no. 103*).

To the East of the county purlins were more often clasped in the 16th century, sometimes with diminished principals. This continued into the 17th century.

In the 18th and early 19th centuries, where the roof of a small house was thatched, softwood pole rafters and even pole purlins and joists were often used (*no. 100*). This was possible because the roofing material was light but these timbers have often been very subject to woodworm. In the 18th century the dormer windows in thatched roofs were usually low 'eyebrow' dormers (*nos. 1 and 16 are typical, 26 is a late example*). At this period the dormer windows of stone and brick buildings with tiled roofs were usually in the roof itself, quite detached from the walls (*nos. 6, 9 and 21*).

No. 103
Tusk tenon purlin joint of the late 18th century. The raking strut to the joint has been reinforced with a later strut. Cottage at Maiden Bradley (a fireplace in this building is shown in no. 58).

The usual roof covering of the 16th century was thatch, or stone tiles were used if the stone of the area would split suitably. Thatch continued in use in many areas until around 1800 after which it was chiefly used by architects for 'picturesque' estate buildings.

Most plain tiles date from the 18th century but they may have been available earlier especially in the Southeast of the county. Pantiles were imported from Somerset in the late 18th and 19th centuries and slates from Wales at the same period, depending chiefly on the river and canal systems for distribution. On stone houses there were often coped parapets at the verges of the roof especially in the late 17th and early 18th centuries, sometimes with decorative kneelers at the eaves (*the front and back covers show early and late examples, also see nos. 11 and 33*).

Garden Features

The earliest garden features which have been found have belonged to manor houses and have dated from the 17th century. They include pillared and arched gateways, gazebos and summerhouses. Dovecotes, stable blocks and granaries were amongst other outbuildings given a decorative appearance but they are beyond the scope of this book.

No. 104
Beeboles of about 1835 in a South-facing brick wall flanking Widbrook Farmhouse, Bradford-on-Avon (no. 27).

Fourteen sets of bee boles, where hives were placed in winter, have so far been found in the county, some through the fieldwork of Wiltshire Buildings Record members. They are described in an article by Anne Foster in the Wiltshire Archaeological Magazine (vol. 80, 1986). They are chiefly situated to the West of the county and appear to date from the 17th century to the early 19th century. Examples are shown in no. 33 and no. 104.

Privies were an important utilitarian feature of gardens but could often also be surprisingly decorative. Evidence of indoor garderobes of 17th century date has been found in a few manor houses but for all social classes the garden privy must have been the normal provision throughout the period covered by this book. Those suspected to be the earliest have been built of rubble stone with stone tiled roofs (*no. 105*) and some have been constructed astride a stream or part of an old moat. There is sometimes a single light or oval window or some kind of arrangement to provide light and ventilation over the doorway. Usually the fittings have been removed and the building survives as a garden shed.

No. 106
Brick privy with plain tiled roof in the garden of a farmhouse at Milton, East Knoyle.

No. 105
Stone privy with stone-tiled roof in the garden of a farmhouse at Easton, Corsham.

Suggested Further Reading

James Ayres 'The Home in Britain' *Faber and Faber* 1981

M. W. Barley 'The English Farmhouse and Cottage' *Routledge and Kegan Paul* 1961

R. W. Brunskill 'Illustrated Handbook of Vernacular Architecture' *Faber and Faber* 1987

John Chandler (*ed.*) 'Studying Wiltshire' *Wiltshire Library and Museum Service* 1982

Pamela Cunnington 'How Old Is Your House' *Alphabooks* 1981

Linda Hall 'The Rural Houses of North Avon and South Gloucestershire 1400–1720' *City of Bristol Museum and Art Gallery (Monograph No. 6)* 1983

Richard Harris 'Discovering Timber-framed Buildings' *Shire Publications* 1979

Barbara Hutton 'Recording Standing Buildings' *Dept. of Archaeology and Prehistory, University of Sheffield and Rescue* 1986

David Iredale 'Discovering Your Old House' *Shire Publications* 1977

Hugh Lander 'House and Cottage Interiors' *Açanthus Books* 1982

E. Mercer 'English Vernacular Houses' *HMSO* 1975

John and Jane Penoyre 'Houses In The Landscape' *Faber and Faber* 1978

Christopher Powell 'Discovering Cottage Architecture' *Shire Publications* 1984

Matthew Saunders 'The Historic Home Owner's Companion' *Batsford* 1987

Lance Smith 'Investigating Old Buildings' *Batsford* 1985

To save space some architectural terms in this book have not been explained in full. The reader is advised to consult Brunskill, Cunnington or Hutton in the list above.

Hall illustrates extended collar roofs and other West Country types. Powell covers cottages built after 1750. Saunders deals with the listing legislation, finance for repairs, the repair of various building materials and features and gives advice on adapting or extending buildings.

Acknowledgements

The Wiltshire Buildings Record is indebted to all the people whose houses are included in this book for their co-operation during recording. Special mention should also be made of Derek Parker who prepared the photographs for printing, Colin Johns who redrew the plans to a common format and Anne Foster who organised the fund-raising. The photographs were taken by Derek Parker, Pamela Slocombe, Peter Treloar, Aubrey Winter, Robin Harvey, Frank Hanford and Peter Filtness. Some additional historical research was undertaken by Robin and Barbara Harvey. We are grateful too for the help of Kenneth Rogers (Wiltshire Record Office), Linda Hall, Avice Wilson and John Reeves (RCHM England) for advice on parts of the text.